Hope Without Measure

*My Cancer Story:
A Journey with
Supernatural Remedies*

Vivien Burgess-Taylor

Contact details: If there is anything in this little book you would like to talk about then please email me at
vivienctaylor@gmail.com
I'm happy to chat.

ℓℙ
www.lifepublications.org.uk

Acknowledgements

Thank You To

Cancer Unit, Mount Vernon Hospital, Middlesex.

Cornerstone Church, Watford for their love and support
both practically and spiritually throughout.

Peta Norman, for being helpful and obedient.

Paul Szkiler, for his recommendation and prayers.

His Place, Germany, for their wonderful Christian love,
support and healing treatments, counselling, prayers and for
just being there!

The late Jean Henderson for her dedication, encouragement
and faithfulness to me daily for two years and beyond.
A true inspiration whom I will never forget.

My extended caring family for always being there for me.

ALL my friends and colleagues for their love, concern,
prayers and positive thoughts.

My wonderful Father God in heaven who was by my side
24/7. He said, *"I will never leave you or forsake you"*.
What a great promise.

I Dedicate This Book To...

Sandy, my wonderful husband,
and dearest son, Matthew,
for their unfailing love and support
in the good times and the bad.
I couldn't have got through it without you!

Commendations

Through this book Vivien will open a door of hope and the tangible power of God to you. If you need healing you will receive healing, if you need deliverance you will get free. Vivien demonstrates that God wants more for you than you want for yourself.

Dr Sharon Stone
CI Europe, Prophetic Voice TV, My Church, Windsor

The power of faith in our invisible God, in life generally and specifically in the realm of healing cannot be underestimated. The amazing belief in what is unseen and has yet to be revealed to the senses, perceiving as real what has yet to become fact is undeniably life giving. Faith has in itself the ability then to inspire hope, another incredible mental and emotional position which, too, carries the potential for healing. When faith and hope are then wrapped in love, love of oneself and of others, and of God, then a mechanism and positioning is in place which has the power to alter one's life trajectory. These three operating together have the ingredients to thwart even the worst diagnosis.

Vivien has embodied faith, hope and love and combined them together with a knowledge of practical nutrition, and has seen for herself as a result the miraculous at work in her own life.

Paul Szkiler
CEO Truestone Impact Investment Management Ltd

I thank Vivien for letting me accompany her on her journey of healing. Every healing building block we found increased healing. The most important thing, she understood the key that healing lies within. Her deep trust in her Creator and power from within restored her.

Carina Summa
Health Care Practitioner, Germany

Contents

Introduction

It's ten years this year, April 2022, since I received my diagnosis and many people who have heard my story have encouraged me to put it into print and so here it is.

As a committed Christian who has a personal relationship with Father God through Jesus, I am writing with this special relationship very much in mind.

This little book has been put together in the hope that it may help and encourage anyone who finds themselves diagnosed with this terrible disease. May it give you peace and hope as you journey with it and to know there can be life after cancer!

Whether you are a Christian, non-Christian, nominal Christian, from another faith, Agnostic, Atheist or just not sure, this little book can be for you!

1

A Shocking Discovery

It was a Wednesday – March 7, 2012 – a day that is imprinted on my memory. About mid morning whilst sitting at my computer, I happened to put my hand up to my neck and there I found a sizeable lump to the right hand side. At first, I thought I was imagining things but had it confirmed when Sandy, my husband, came into the home office where I was working and saw it for himself.

I knew generally, that lumps were not good things to find on one's body and took no time in calling my GP's surgery and was able to get an appointment for that afternoon. The doctor I saw gave me a little bit of encouragement as he thought it was nothing to worry about, but he would send me to get a biopsy for peace of mind. I left there believing he was right and all would be well as I was feeling very well in myself, again I felt it was confirmation that what the doctor said was correct.

The next day I had a biopsy where they withdrew fluid from the lump through a syringe.

The following Tuesday, whilst parking my car to get some shopping after finishing work, my mobile rang. I noticed the number was the doctor's surgery and thought they only phone with good news right? How wrong could I be!

The doctor asked me where I was, I told him, "I've just parked up". He apologised for calling me on my mobile but said, "I'm afraid I'm not calling with good news. Your results are back and you have Lymphoma." I went from feeling optimistic to just being numb and shaky.

Eventually, when I was able to speak I said, "Could you repeat that please?" which he did, explaining, depending on which kind of Lymphoma I had, I had a fifty/fifty chance of survival. He went on to explain this was why he was phoning me rather than inviting me to the surgery, because he wanted to "get things moving" and for me to see a Haematologist as soon as possible.

I left the car to continue with my shopping and to be honest I got the items I needed and drove home to tell my husband and son the news in a complete daze. Thinking back now, I really don't think I should have been driving! I just wanted to get home to speak to someone! At that time my husband Sandy and son Matthew worked together in an office at the end of our garden.

When I got home and went into the house it was to find the office and house empty, both had gone out. I sat down in a chair in the lounge still in a daze saying over and over to myself, "I have cancer, I have cancer".

Saying the "C" word just did not make sense, it all seemed so surreal because I didn't think there was any way I could ever have cancer. Maybe they had made a mistake was another thought or I possibly misheard the doctor. Did I really have that conversation? All these different thoughts and more were going on in my head as I tried to take it all in.

It wasn't long before I heard the front door opening and both the men in my life returning in a buoyant mood. That soon changed when they entered the lounge to find me sitting there still with my jacket on.

"What's wrong with you," they laughed! All I could say was, "I am sorry, I am sorry". "What are you on about?" was the reply. Then I told them the news. There was silence, before Sandy, said, "Are you sure you didn't pick the doctor up wrong?"

I shared with them the whole sequence of events. They both tried to re-assure me as best they could, but I couldn't respond as I was still trying to process everything. It was not only me trying to process it but now it was also my family. We mustn't forget our partners and family in all this.

I broke the news to my sisters, who were both obviously shocked but very supportive, and they in turn told the extended family. The one person I was really concerned about telling was my dear Mum but that was taken out of my hands too.

Part of my Christian faith when one gets sick or unwell is to ask the elders of the church to pray and anoint the sick person with oil. It just so happened that it was Tuesday, and the elders of our church were meeting that evening. Nothing is a coincidence with God. So that evening I was prayed for and anointed with oil as instructed in scripture, the Bible. I also renounced any foreign body within me. That night I actually slept quite well.

The following morning I picked up my Bible and I asked God (well actually I cried out to God) to show me something from His word, the Bible, so that I knew He was hearing me and to give me hope. My Bible opened in the Psalms and I turned over the page and there in front of me was Psalm 91. Now, I had read this Psalm many times before but that day it took on a whole different meaning for me.

Each verse was telling me of God's protection over me and then came the final verse, *"With long life I will satisfy him and give him my salvation!"*

I thanked God there and then for hearing and answering me and I believed that Psalm was the beginning of knowing I was heading for something good. However, it also says in this Psalm you won't get any of these things unless you put your trust completely in God. This was something I knew I had to do. He has the supernatural power.

I realised that as I believed in the power of prayer, I needed it more now than ever. So, I began to call people I knew who would pray for me in a positive way, from the north of Scotland right down to the south of England. Then I went international and, in the end, had people in eight different countries praying for me! All this I believe was medicine for my healing.

2

Diagnosis – My Journey Begins

The following week, I received a call from our local hospital offering me an appointment that week to see a Haematologist.

I went along to the appointment accompanied by my husband Sandy (Sandy attended every appointment and treatment with me throughout my whole journey, he never left my side) in fear and trepidation not sure what I was going to hear.

I cannot describe clearly what goes on in one's head when going to these appointments. You are trying to keep positive because that is what you want to hear, positive news, but at the end of the day it is fear – the worst-case scenario – that is driving you.

Fortunately, I didn't have to wait long and I was introduced to one of the loveliest men I could hope to find, especially in circumstances I found myself. He immediately put me at ease. He told me there were various lymphomas, all curable bar one, but he couldn't say I had lymphoma at that point without a proper biopsy taken surgically from the lump on my neck, more bloods taken and another full body scan.

On the same day, following his appointment, I was taken to another unit at the hospital and there had the biopsy and bloods taken. Within a week I was back and had a CAT scan.

As I was waiting for these results, it had been arranged that I would travel to Scotland (we live in the South of England), to celebrate my Mum's 90th birthday on April 2, (we had lost Dad to cancer four months earlier).

I decided to continue with this commitment, and after consultation with my sisters we felt it best to delay telling Mum my diagnosis until after her birthday. I didn't want to put a dampener on her celebrations in any way.

My time up there was lovely celebrating with Mum, but I found it quite difficult being with the rest of my family. They were loving, caring and supportive but as the future journey was uncertain, I felt very unsettled and of course upset. I tried not to show it but what was going on inside was a different story.

A week later, when all the celebrations were over and after a telephone call with Brenda, my sister and Mum's carer, it was decided she would go and tell Mum herself rather than me telling her over the phone. When she did this, obviously Mum was shocked and upset but Mum being Mum very soon became resilient and practical as she always did with everything that life threw at her right up to her death at 98 years of age.

When I received that first phone call from her after hearing my news, I really was surprised how strong and positive she was. You see, I was always Mum's "baby" as my two sisters, Ruth and Brenda, are ten and twelve years older than me. We did spend some time crying together but very soon she was bucking me up with wonderful and encouraging words.

My times speaking with Mum and sisters Ruth and Brenda were certainly difficult for me but I'm sure just as difficult for them too. I can't thank them enough for their support, even although it was from many miles away, I knew they were there for me.

After sharing my news with my Mum life continued as near to normal as possible under these circumstances for the next month, when I received a call from the Haematologist to say they had all the results back and would I come and see him that week on the Friday.

On arrival, he came out of his room and asked me to follow him over to another part of the hospital where it was quieter. It did seem a bit strange, but I thought maybe it's just the way they do things when they are giving results. Little did I expect what he was about to tell me!

After we were seated, he told me he was very sorry, the results had come back and I didn't have lymphoma but lung cancer. There was a tumour on a lymph gland behind my sternum, but the good news was, my lungs were clear and there was no evidence of disease in any other part of my body. The biopsy had shown strains of lung cancer and therefore they had to treat me for that. This diagnosis was considered to be quite rare and was now outside his expertise and I was transferred to see an Oncologist the following Monday, which happened to be on my birthday.

I left that room devastated but hopeful at the same time. It was good it was contained and my lungs were clear. Wasn't it?

That weekend was a peculiar one as we tried to get our heads around this latest news but also continuing to be hopeful and trying to carry on living as normally as we could.

Monday arrived and after spending time praying we very nervously went along to the hospital to see the Oncologist. Again, still being hopeful as we were holding on to and believing in God's promises.

We were blessed that the church we attended at that time was just opposite the hospital and we were able to park in their car park. As we pulled into the car park Richard, the Pastor, just happened to come out of the church and was able to pray with us before we went across to the hospital. No words uttered go unheard and I was so grateful for all the prayers that went up on my behalf around this time.

It was a very strange set-up at Watford General Hospital where I attended for the clinics. We waited in the waiting area before being called, to then go through and sit and wait in a long line before our turn came. What we were actually sitting in were porta cabins with no soundproofing and this was the clinic set up for cancer patients!

As you can imagine, you are nervous enough as it is but to be able to hear everyone else's conversation and diagnosis behind closed doors, did not at all help no matter how hard you tried to close your ears to what was being said. And then to watch patients leave these rooms in distraught states was very upsetting to say the least. Hence, another very good reason not to want to go to these clinic appointments. I just dreaded the whole scenario.

Eventually, we were called in to meet the Oncologist who spoke with a Scottish accent and as I am also Scottish I thought great, we should get on well here, we have something in common. Unfortunately, that did not prove to be the case!

We sat down and she went over the results of the scans. She explained that whereas my original diagnosis of Lymphoma was possibly curable, the situation I found myself in now was not, and all they could do was try and contain it. An operation was also out of the question because of where the tumour was. The first thing on offer was chemotherapy and that would need to start in two to three weeks' time. All this was communicated to us in a very brusque and uncaring way. What a great birthday present!

Sandy thought treatment might happen more quickly if we went down the private route but when he asked her the question, he was very rudely "put down" and told, "If you want good looking nurses and fancy wallpaper, you go private." We both sat there looking at each other but I had so much going around in my head trying to take in all that had been said, I sat there again just numb.

I remember we were then taken to another room to speak to a MacMillan nurse and go over things with her; don't ask me what because by this stage I was like a zombie and not registering much. I remember saying to her, "I don't want to be in pain…will I be in pain?" I had seen people with lung disease before and they can struggle quite a lot. She assured me all would be done to keep me out of as much pain as possible. That didn't really answer the question…

After all the formalities, I left that room and walked the length of the corridor of the porta cabin out into the hospital corridors and back to the car with legs like jelly and numbness, that's the only way to describe how I felt. Driving home felt surreal, looking around at things I saw mostly every day, wondering how much longer I had to see them.

I continued daily to speak Psalm 91 over myself, and I personalised it to make it more real. I thanked God for giving it to me.

3

Treatment

As the days and weeks progressed word had got around of the change in my circumstance and I was inundated with phone calls, cards, letters, flowers and of course prayers. Each one was so appreciated and the kind, encouraging words said to me, about myself, overwhelmed me! I can tell you lots of tears were shed as I read and listened to the many words of encouragement and love.

Our Pastor Richard called and prayed with us and there was an all-night prayer meeting arranged at our church. Unfortunately, at that time, there were five of us in the church diagnosed with cancer and it wasn't a large congregation. It was felt that there was an attack from the evil one on the church and so we had to go into warfare mode with our prayers. This was done with passion. How I appreciated the love and support from that little church.

During the days and weeks following my diagnosis I began to think much about heaven. What will it be like? Who will I see first? Will Dad be waiting at the portal for me? My first words to him would be, "Bet you didn't expect to see me so soon Dad!" Or, will the first person I see be Jesus? What will He say to me? What will I say to Him? I think I will just be in awe. The more I imagined the more excited I became when

I realised, very soon, I could be seeing Jesus who I put my trust in many years ago! However, there was the other side of me that wanted to live here for a little while longer.

Up to this point I was still working at my lovely job as office manager in a stained-glass studio. However, when I was given my diagnosis, I went into the office and just knew that I couldn't carry on working as I just was not able to concentrate. My boss was very gracious and let me go saying, "Come back when you are ready". The wonderful staff that I worked with wouldn't let a temp come in and took on my role as well as their own and covered my job for me. I was so touched and can't thank them enough for their support and love during and after that time, to the present day. We will remain a true family.

The days and weeks went by and after four weeks from my last appointment with the Oncologist, I hadn't heard anything about starting my chemotherapy treatment, I very reluctantly phoned to find out what was happening. As I was feeling quite well, carrying on with life as normal, I did not cherish the thought of having chemotherapy, so I kept putting off contacting them. I actually began to feel that they might have got it wrong and it was gone.

I eventually got through to my allocated Macmillan nurse. After asking her when I was going to hear about a date to start treatment, she said, "Well, in your case there is no urgency". To this day, I don't know what she meant because I didn't want to ask her to find out. I took the positive side thinking; it can't be that bad so they are not in a hurry. However, I hadn't forgotten what the Oncologist told me, I needed to start treatment within three weeks.

I continued to keep myself busy, seeing many of my great friends who watched out for me and took me out for lots of coffees and lunches. Those little things to them were big things for me as they helped keep my mind occupied. I found it was very easy at home to become morose and feel sorry for myself and of course I believe the evil one (the devil) loved using those times to fill me with fear. I have to say he won many times in my fragile state.

After church one Sunday evening, whilst waiting to hear a date to start treatment, a lovely lady in our church, Jean, a real woman of God, prayed for me after the service. As she laid her hand on me I could feel a burning sensation going right through my body. I just felt this was a touch from the Holy Spirit. I shared this with her and she asked me if she could be my prayer partner on this journey. Of course, I said yes, nobody had asked me this before and I felt it a joy and privilege to have Jean walk with me through this time, as I didn't know then what lay ahead.

Eventually, six weeks later, I received an appointment to begin chemotherapy at Mount Vernon Hospital.

Two weeks before this, however, I received a phone call from a lady who just happened to be at a prayer group a few miles away from where we live. My name happened to come up for prayer and she recognised my name as she was a friend of a friend of mine. She explained to me that she had been looking into alternative treatments for cancer and told me about a particular treatment based on a special diet, but they did not recommend chemotherapy or radiotherapy.

I listened but to be honest a lot went over my head as I knew I was starting chemo in two weeks' time, not only that it would be a massive decision to turn down chemo that might help me and I knew nothing about this diet apart from what Peta was telling me.

By the end of the call Peta was telling me about a gentleman who had started on this diet, had cancer in various places, was now clear and was local. My ears pricked up when I heard this. She very kindly gave me his number to speak to him. I thank Peta to this day for taking the time to call me for that chat. Little did I know then what impact this special diet would have on my life.

After the call I spoke with Sandy. Up to this point, I was very cynical about natural therapies, but there was something niggling at me, it could be a good thing – I was quite confused. His advice was, you don't close doors until you go through, and to investigate with prayer.

I called the gentleman whose number I was given, who was very helpful and explained what he did and where he got what was needed. It wasn't just what you ate but the many supplements and potions you needed to take as well. I was really encouraged after talking to him – humanly speaking, it gave me hope.

It took a few days, but I made the decision to have the chemo treatment and whilst going through it I would research this diet I had been told about.

A few days before commencing the treatment, I had a visit from a colleague of Sandy's. He was a lovely young man who two years previously, himself, had to have chemotherapy and was completely well. He gave me good advice, before he had each treatment he would repeat a line from a verse in the Bible that *"when they drink deadly poison, it will not hurt them at all" (Mark 16:18).* I kept this in my mind.

At this point I should mention our wonderful son Matthew. Matthew was obviously very upset with my diagnosis but Matthew being Matthew began to research firstly Lymphoma and then lung cancer. He's a great researcher. One of the things Matthew found out about was cannabis and how good it was – especially for sickness during chemo.

He came to me and said, "Mum, I want to come with you the next time you visit the doctor". And he did. He told the doctor he knew cannabis was very good for pain and sickness during chemo and he knew where to get some. He didn't want his mum to suffer in any way if there was something known to work. This was before CBD oil or anything like that was openly available.

The GP was very gracious and explained to Matthew that there were various things they could try first, but he would keep it in mind and knew where to find him. We never did go down the cannabis route however.

Matthew was a constant support to me and his dad at this time. I now know that Matthew did struggle very much emotionally with the whole scenario, but like many men, he didn't show it and in many ways is still suffering from the consequences today. We do have to think about the carers in these circumstances too and not just the sufferer. Both these men, who I love dearly, are a constant in my life and I could never have got through it without all that they did for me.

Another friend came to visit and before leaving gave me a book on healing which he had found very useful. I began to read this little book and very quickly it became second to my Bible as a resource. It was full of verses from the Bible on God's promises for our healing. It explained how to ask and believe in healing. I learned new things from this little book and I would pray the verses over myself each day, sometimes numerous times, believing the words I was saying, and this made me much more positive in my heart that I was going to be healed. It was my "go to" book if I felt a bit down in the dumps. And I still use it today.

The week before I was due to start treatment, I was invited to attend the Lynda Jackson Macmillan Centre at the hospital to go over the treatment, discuss how we may feel and ways to look after ourselves during the treatment. There I met Elizabeth, we were going to start our treatments together. She was an older lady who was very frightened. We had a chat and I said, "We're in this together so we can support one another". She asked me how I was so at peace and I was able to share with her it was God through Jesus and prayer but that fear did creep in from time to time. Elizabeth was a Roman Catholic and had prayed to one of the saints who she believed would help her on her journey. It was good we met, and we had each other as support.

I also was invited to the hospital for a PET scan the week before treatment, which is a deep full body scan. More about that later.

And so the day arrived, it was a Thursday in May 2012, Sandy and I left for Mount Vernon Hospital to arrive for 9am. I was to be there the full day and overnight for each treatment. Naturally, I was very apprehensive, worried and scared all rolled into one!

During our day at the Lynda Jackson Centre, we were given a brief tour round the ward we would be in for our treatment. It was difficult not to notice there were some very ill patients and it was a real concern for me as I didn't know how I would cope having to watch these poor patients. In normal circumstances, it would not have phased me, but the fear element meant I could end up like some of these people and to be honest, I did not want to go there and even think that way.

We were welcomed by a lovely nurse at the door to the ward and after the usual checking-in procedure she said, "Follow me". We started to walk up the ward and about halfway I looked to my left and there was someone I recognised, just an acquaintance but a lovely Christian lady, and realised immediately she was very ill. I found it quite upsetting to see how this vicious disease can completely devastate one's body as I saw the effects of it in front of me.

We carried on walking and were taken to the rear of the ward and ushered into a private room with en-suite. I hesitated as I thought they had made a mistake but was assured that as there was no room on the ward I would have this lovely room to myself. For me this was an answer to prayer! I believe that God knew how I was feeling and how much I could cope with and rescued me from that situation. As I was settling in, I looked across the corridor to the room opposite and who was sitting there but Elizabeth!

Once I got settled, I wandered across to have a chat with Elizabeth and her two daughters. That was the start of a good friendship for some of that season. When the evening came and our family left to go home, Elizabeth and I would get together for a chat and encourage one another and try and have a laugh. It so happened every three weeks, when we had to have our next treatment of chemo, it was arranged for the same day, so we could see each other again.

And so, after all the relevant blood tests had been taken and results obtained, the lab got the go-ahead to make up my "concoction". I was given a pre-solution for about one hour intravenously and then the big yellow bag of chemo arrived, £6,000 worth I was told, (and that was ten years ago) which took, if I remember rightly, six to eight hours to slowly drip into my body. Following that there was then another hour or two of saline. I'm sure there was more but couldn't tell you what they were. As you can imagine I didn't get much sleep with many trips to the loo!

As I was hooked up to the big yellow bag, I remembered a verse from the Bible I had been given a few weeks previously, *"no deadly poison shall harm you"* (Mark 16:18), and so I kept repeating these words over and over from time to time, as I watched the solution enter my body.

Later that evening, when the night staff came on duty, I was dozing and then heard someone come into my room. When I opened my eyes I saw a nurse at the end of my bed who just happened to be a near neighbour from our village and we both recognised each other. I'm not sure who was more shocked. It was lovely having Vanda there to chat to and she was such a great encouragement each time I had my treatment. God is good.

It felt like a real treat when early in the morning between 7am-8am the nurses would come in and remove the drip and canula from my arm and give me a nice cup of tea and some toast. As soon as 9am arrived Sandy would walk in ready to take me home.

After the first round of chemo, apart from feeling very tired so I slept a lot, I felt quite good and thought if this is it then it should be a dawdle. By the time the next round was due three weeks later, I felt more energised and able to cope much better. Little did I know!

And so round two began. I went through exactly the same procedure at the hospital as round one. Again, straight to the rear of the ward to my own room with Elizabeth opposite.

Now as I said, before I started any chemotherapy they had given me a PET scan. This is a very deep full body scan and just before I started this second cycle of chemo, I had a visit from my Oncologist to give me the results, I have to say that she was a lot more pleasant this time and even sat on the end of my bed for a little chat. Wow!

She proceeded to tell me that the cancer was now in my liver and in the bone on my spine in two places. I was speechless. Remember instead of three weeks, I waited six weeks to begin treatment! Sandy asked her what the prognosis was, but she couldn't tell him at that stage. Although I knew this was not good news, I have to say I had this amazing peace resting over me and of course I had something they didn't know about...a diet!

No sooner had she left when we heard feet running up the ward and two nurses came flying into the room and stopped abruptly. They looked at me and asked if I was ok. I said, "Yes". "But you have just been given bad news," they replied. They obviously expected to see me very upset. I told them I was a committed Christian and was believing my God for healing.

As much as I was depending on the chemo to do its work and really appreciated everything they were doing for me, I was depending on God more as He is the Greatest Physician.

We chatted and they said from experience, people who have faith generally make a better recovery. To hear that was a great comfort.

As Sandy was leaving that evening he stood at the end of the bed, looked at me and said, "We're going to get through this," and assured me that whatever decisions I made he would be behind me 100 per cent. I knew together we would give it a blooming good try with the main source of help from above, of course!

Once back home, however, I felt much more tired than round one and by day two started to experience continual nausea. Then during the night the vomiting began, so much so we had to call the on-call doctor out as we were concerned I would get dehydrated. He gave me an injection to stop the vomiting which worked very quickly, and I was able to sleep. Unfortunately, when the injection began to wear off, back came the nausea. This cycle continued and my GP tried various anti-sickness tablets, but it took until the fourth and last chemo session to get the right medication and dose to take effect.

Word had reached some of Sandy's business colleagues about my illness and one in particular, who lived in France, contacted us recommending a natural supplement they used over there for cancer to help with chemotherapy. This was sent to me to try as well, and it proved helpful. People were so loving and caring.

Between the sickness and the effect of chemo on my body, I began to feel very weak and lethargic. It wasn't long before I had great difficulty climbing the stairs and on one occasion Sandy had to more or less carry me up. This feeling was very debilitating, and I found myself unable to think, pray, read and on some occasions even to speak, the weakness was so great. It also left me very emotional and on my own I would let the flood gates open and let the tears flow. I would cry out to God for help.

People were very kind between messaging and phoning, but I found myself unable to speak to or message them, again because of the weakness. My body felt drained and I moved around the house like a zombie, so Sandy and Matthew had to speak for me. Visitors were off the cards too as there was no way I could hold a conversation.

4

No Coincidences with God

"In sickness and in health" was our commitment to each other many years previously, and Sandy proved to be my constant support, he helped me get up in the morning and get dressed. I did manage to have a bath each day, as I was unable to stand for any length of time so couldn't shower. Even then, he would be on "standby" if I was unable to get myself out of the bath, fortunately that never happened.

During the night when the fear would come and take over, (it always seemed worse at night, as most things do), I would often wake him up and say "pray" and of course he would, he understood why. This would happen at times during the day too, and each time Sandy prayed I would receive a great peace to sleep or carry on my day. God promises to give us *"a peace that passes all understanding"* and that's exactly what I experienced.

At this point I should mention my GP who was a fantastic support throughout my illness. At one point I wasn't feeling very well, and I called him. It was a Friday, and we had a chat on the phone mid-afternoon. He decided to leave things as they were and see how I was after the weekend.

At 7pm that evening there was a knock on the door, this was my lovely doctor on his way home from the surgery. "I just wanted to come and see you for myself and make sure you're ok", he said. I was so surprised but touched at this as I'm afraid not many doctors these days would do something like that, especially on their way home on a Friday evening! Such was his dedication. I felt really blessed.

Again, the third treatment was the same procedure as before and again another room on my own. You couldn't make it up. God is so good. Not once did I request it.

However, this time there was no Elizabeth. I'm not sure what happened but I knew from the previous session, her body was beginning to struggle with the chemotherapy. To this day I don't know what happened but what I do know, whilst we were together, we were there for each other, and I will always remember our little chats together. She was a lovely lady.

I had four chemotherapy treatments in total and after each session, by the third week I would begin to feel a little better and stronger, then wham, crash back down again as another dose of chemo hit my body.

Our church ladies were marvellous, they got together and provided cooked meals for us as a family, our freezer was bulging. We would get a message to say there is some food on your doorstep and we would open the door to all this wonderful freshly cooked food. Our cleaner took on extra duties to help Sandy because he still had to work. Fortunately, he has his own business and as said before, works from an office in our garden which was very helpful, and our son Matthew works in the business, so both were on hand if needed. Again, I feel it a real blessing to have had them so close to hand for that time.

I went for my fourth and final treatment, but this time was slightly different in that I wasn't taken to the rear of the ward but to the first bed on the right as you entered the ward. Oh no! This was something I was dreading. I sat on the edge of the bed and looked around. I had two elderly ladies opposite me, a lady of similar age to myself next to me and diagonally opposite again was a lady of similar age to myself. The rest of the ward was quiet.

I settled myself into my bed and waited for all the procedures to begin. The lady next to me slept most of the time before being taken away for tests. The doctors arrived to see one of the elderly ladies and the curtains were pulled round. Now you might not see what is going on, but you can certainly hear what is being said and this was something I found very difficult to cope with. This poor lady was being given bad news, but the full ward could hear.

Afterwards, I felt so sorry for her, and she was obviously very upset. During the night the other elderly lady opposite was taken into a side ward, and her family were called.

And so the procedure began again with myself, all the various blood tests taken to see if my body would withstand yet another round of chemo and the good news was it could. It didn't take long for all this liquid being pumped into my body to react naturally and having no en-suite this time, I had to walk the length of the ward to visit the loo trailing my chemo bag stand with me. What a palaver this whole procedure was, as you can imagine, and so, I would hold on as long as I could before making such visits.

On my way back from one of those visits at about 4am, I noticed the lady who was diagonally opposite me awake and sitting on the edge of her bed. We both smiled at each other, and I made my way over and spoke to her very quietly so as not to wake anyone. She was unable to sleep as she was concerned regarding the outcome of tests, she had been told her bowel cancer had returned after five years. She was waiting to hear what the next stage in the procedure would be. This lady came from another town in Hertfordshire and her husband would come in daily to sit with her and she commented to me how nice it was to see Sandy sitting with me too and we both realised how blessed we were as not many would be able to do that because of their employment.

We sat for a couple of hours chatting, with the nurses supplying us with cups of tea and biscuits. She was a lovely lady; we were of similar age, and we just seemed to hit it off and had a lot in common. I was able to share my faith with her and she was keen to know more and had a lot of questions. I often wonder what happened to her.

The following morning about 9am the ward went from a room of quiet and calm to a noise level that seemed, quite honestly, to be nearly off the scale. It started with the arrival of one or two ladies who were delighted to see each other with around another four or five who took over the rear of the ward to have their "chemo party" as it was one of the group's birthdays. Apparently, they would make sure they booked their chemo treatments together, get hooked up and have fun! Out came the cakes and candles, they even had music, I'm not sure what was drank…but I'm sure whatever it was, it would have been allowed!

Yes, this is quite common apparently, some ladies would throw "chemo parties", but for me personally, I couldn't get my head round it. It's the last thing I could think of. However, if it helped them cope then who am I to say anything? I don't know how other very ill patients could have coped with the disturbance but I'm sure the staff would have it in hand. For me, I was just glad to be going home that day.

Another thing that perplexed me whilst there was the number of people who continued to go outside in their dressing gowns hooked up to their chemo stands to have their cigarettes. Especially after been told how much my chemo cost I really thought it would make people think, but certainly at that time, there were many who didn't or wouldn't. It was obvious their lifestyle wasn't going to change. For me, it's something I just don't understand.

And so, this was my last chemo session at Mount Vernon Hospital. Whoop! Whoop!

Just before leaving the ward a lovely young Muslim lady, her name escapes me, came over and had a chat. She said to me, "Where do you get your peace from?" It was an unusual question I thought, but I was able to explain to her that I put my trust in Jesus as He died on the cross for forgiveness of sins as well as healing, and because of that I had to believe I would be healed. He tells us to, "ask, believe and receive". She listened and said she prayed to God and believed the same. Now I know her God and my God may be different, but she was happy to listen and then asked me if I would pray for her uncle in Canada named Kasim, a young man, who had a brain tumour and was very ill. Of course, I said I would, and we did, but we never did find out anymore but continued to pray for him daily for four or five months.

All these moments I believe were God ordained. He put me in that place at that time for a reason. Again, I say it, nothing is a coincidence with God. Is it a place I would like to return to? Definitely not. However, looking back, I can see how God had His hand on me through every stage of the journey and no stage was wasted. I am so grateful to all the staff that looked after me so graciously and I admire each one of them for their dedication to their vocation and patients. It takes a very special person to do what thcy do.

5

My New Diet

I now was home but couldn't say I was looking forward to the future because I didn't know what I was looking forward to, if that makes sense. I knew spiritually but not physically. Yes, I was believing but I still had no prognosis from the medical profession which in many ways I was glad of, but I made up my mind I had to declare my healing and keep believing. This I did with the help and encouragement of friends and family but especially my good friend and prayer partner Jean Henderson.

Now some days were better than others on my recovery path. Did I get my miserable "down" days? I certainly did. The devil is alive and well and he was doing his utmost to bring me down – the feeling of dejection, feeling sorry for myself and just being generally low. It didn't help that I was still very weak from the treatment, and this remained for a few months after finishing my chemo.

At this point, I want to mention more about my dear friend Jean. Jean was a powerful prayer warrior and when she asked if she could be my prayer partner I was delighted. Every morning at 9.15am I would get a text message from Jean. It could be a verse of scripture, a song or hymn or just encouraging words and I can honestly say that whatever it was, it was always spot on for me for that day! Again, no coincidence. This she did every day for two years, even when she went on holiday such was her love, devotion and dedication. If I was feeling really low, it would be a phone call, or she would visit. Nothing was ever too much trouble.

Sadly, we lost Jean on July 16, 2021, ironically to cancer. She has left a big void in my life, and I miss her immensely, but I know because of our faith, we will be reunited one day, and I can't wait to meet her again. She has been a true inspiration, and I will never forget how she supported me in so many ways and what she did for me. She was so faithful.

A few weeks after I finished my treatment, a colleague of Sandy's from Surrey was telling his neighbour (who we've never met) over the fence, about our situation, and on hearing this he immediately offered us the use of their apartment in Swanage, Dorset, to use anytime. So, it was arranged, we went there for a week a few weeks later, although still quite weak it was lovely to sit by the sea and have short walks around Swanage. People's kindness was overwhelming.

When I had my good moments, I would undertake research into the Budwig Diet that I was told about before I had started my treatment. I began to buy and send for various supplements, powders and potions that were recommended for the type of cancer I had.

The plan was, when I felt strong enough, to begin very slowly by taking what was suggested for my new diet. When I say diet, this was not to lose weight but a new healthy way of eating, only taking into your body the purest of food and drink you can get. It was an anti-cancer diet. This was very much a hit or miss as my appetite was all over the place and I still had certain cravings, a side effect of the chemo. So I just did what I could for several weeks. The first thing I did was to cut out sugar and dairy as both these feed tumours. I was very strict with this one. After a couple of weeks or so I would introduce something else into the diet. This gave time for my body to adjust to this new way of eating and drinking.

I can remember the first time I tried a drink I was sent. It was simply a powder mixed with water. Sandy very kindly mixed it for me the first time I tried it first thing in the morning on an empty stomach and still in bed. I think I had two mouthfuls and as soon as it hit my stomach, up it came. Oh boy, was I sick. I remember feeling quite upset afterwards as I thought my body was rejecting it and I would never be able to progress with this diet that I felt I was given for a purpose and was going to be part of my healing programme. I wasn't going to be beaten, however, and so a couple of days later, I got up and mixed the concoction myself. I sat down with the sick bowl beside me just in case. Very gingerly I sipped the liquid, so far so good, little by little I took sips until I had finished it. And I waited and waited. Praise God the sick bowl wasn't needed! That was the start of the Budwig Diet for me.

I continued with that for at least two years adding new foods, drinks and supplements as I went and making changes along the way. In fact, to this day, I still use some of it in my diet although over the years it has changed.

6

A Promise from God

Six weeks had gone by and now it was time for my first scan since finishing the chemo. This would tell me if the chemo had worked and what was the way forward. I had a CT scan and then went to see the Oncologist a week later.

Again, I went to the clinic in fear and trepidation, obviously concerned about the results but also how this lady was going to react today and what sort of mood would she be in, all this was going on in my head.

I was invited into her room and there she was sitting in front of her computer. It seemed an age before she spoke but when she did she asked me how I was and how I had coped with the chemo etc. She then said, "Well, I have good news, the chemo has done its job and reduced everything by 50 per cent." "Great!" I thought. She then proceeded to say that they could do no more for me as the chemo had done its job so all they could do now was monitor me and just hope for the best, but the outcome didn't look good. It would eventually be terminal but again she couldn't give a prognosis. No, this was not going to happen!

I left that room deflated in one sense but excited in another, it was really strange. I never to this day told her about the diet

I was given as I know how the medical profession in general feels about natural therapy, although I think they are becoming more accepting of natural alternatives. I walked along the corridor thinking to myself, but you don't know what I'm doing and I'm going to show you! It was as if someone was willing me on and I think my determination really kicked in at that point. From then on, I just looked forward to the day when I would have a scan and they could say, there is no cancer.

The following morning, as I sat on the edge of my bed, my mind still like mush because of "chemo brain", I had what I can only describe as near as possible to hearing the audible voice of God. It was so loud in my head; I heard the words, *"I have begun a good work in you"*.

I knew these were words from a verse in the Bible and just at that point Sandy walked into the room and I told him what I had just heard. He said, "And what does the rest of that verse say? *'and I will carry it out to completion'"*. Notice the word *"will"*, not might or maybe (Philippians 1:6). I believe that this was God speaking to me through His Holy Spirit and I knew then that this was confirmation I was going to be made completely well. It reminded me of Psalm 91 which I was given the first day I was diagnosed, I had to put my trust entirely in God and He would do the rest.

I can remember walking around the house speaking to God, (if anyone saw me they would think I had lost the plot…) and thanking Him for my healing which I believed had already happened because He said, in the Bible, *"by my stripes you are healed"*, along with many more promises for healing, but my body just didn't know it yet.

I would walk around saying, "Thank you, thank you, thank you for providing my healing at Calvary, I *am* healed," declaring it out loud over and over. Deep inside me, I can only describe it as a feeling of real joy mixed with excitement as I realised I was healed and couldn't wait to hear it from the medical profession, so I had proof.

People would ask me how I was and I would tell them I was fine, and I was healed. Some said "great", others would look at me as if I was on another planet. Yes, I have to say, many were Christians and I have to say as well that their reactions quite often were ones of disappointment for me when they would then ask, "But how are you really?"

Even if the conversation was on the phone there would be silence at the other end. This taught me a lesson, because I am sure I'd said the same thing myself many times. However, I would very quickly pick myself up and kept on declaring! I would keep saying to myself, "If God gave all these promises, He didn't give them for nothing." I had to keep believing.

And so I continued with the Budwig Diet, kept to it religiously and continued to lose weight. This was becoming concerning to me. Was it the chemo? Was it the diet? Was it both together? Or was it the disease? I just wasn't used to looking in the mirror and seeing a slim or should I say skinny Vivien! My whole life I have been on and off diets, so to see myself so thin I couldn't cope with it really, good on one front but not so good on another and not the nicest way to lose weight either!

However, I knew if I was to get well, I would need to give myself a chance and keep to this very strict diet, eating lots of good things and cutting out all the bad from my diet. I managed to do this over time – just cutting out the bad very gradually so my body could get used to it slowly.

Was it hard? Yes, it was. Did I struggle at times? Yes, I did. But I kept saying to myself, "It's a small price to pay". If this was the only sacrifice I had to make, well then it would be worth it.

Not only was it what I ate, but I had also so many supplements, powders, tinctures and potions to take, my life had to be very organised. This wasn't a real problem for me as I'm generally a very organised person, so I just got on with it. At one time I counted 34 supplements I was taking per day. Then there were all the powders, tinctures and so on, and they all had to be taken at certain times of the day, some together some not. Did I get out? Not a lot. When I did, I had to take what I needed with me. It was quite a palaver at times. If need be, I would physically take them in the car or in bathrooms. I usually knew where I was going and would organise myself around that.

I have to say, in a matter of three months, I had much of my energy back, the aches and pains I suffered before and during my treatment had nearly gone. I still got tired but that was gradually getting less and less as time went on.

I went for a walk each day, starting with a few metres down the road, then gradually to the end of the road and I remember the day well when I walked to the café a few streets away and met up with friends Jean and Heather, who instead of coming to see me at home met me in the café. This, for me, was a great milestone and I was really chuffed when I arrived and didn't feel in any way tired. They insisted on giving me a lift back home though. This was the start I believe of my real recovery.

This meeting up became a regular occurrence when weekly we met for coffee and then one day, we went a little further afield and didn't just have coffee but lunch as well. Eventually, we were often out for most of the day, depending on where we were going. This was the start of a close friendship between the three of us which continued for nine years, until Jean was taken from us. Heather and I continue to meet regularly and often reminisce about our times with dear Jean.

7

Off to Germany

It was time for another scan at the hospital. It was about three months since the previous one. I had the scan and went to the hospital for the results. Once in the consultant's room, she then proceeded to say, "I have good news for you," Mrs Taylor, "your sternum is clear and your liver is clear but there's still disease in your spine!" Wow! Wow! I thanked her very much and left that room on a high but also thanking God for giving me this special diet. It seemed to be working! Of course, not letting on to her what I was doing.

I was still very conscious that although I was getting stronger, I still had disease to deal with in my spine. Just after I finished chemotherapy, I had one session of radiotherapy on my spine which left me for a few months with back discomfort. There was a visible indent on my spine and an area seemed distorted

One of Sandy's closest friends was Paul and they met up weekly. One week Paul had just returned from Germany where he had taken his son to a Christian Wellness Centre. He told Sandy that they were seeing great results with healings from different diseases and cancers, and he really felt quite strongly that I should go there. So, Sandy came home and relayed the message. What was my instant reaction? *There's no way I'm going all the way to Germany to somewhere I know nothing about, and it will cost a lot of money.* Again, that was the old negative Vivien coming out. Sandy said, "We don't close doors until we go through and investigate, let's go for a few days and find out more about it". I couldn't really argue with that, so it was arranged. Off to Germany we went.

I was asked if I would like to make an appointment to see the Health Care Practioner before I went or wait until I arrived. Of course, I said, wait until we arrive. I didn't know what I was going to nor what it was all about, being a typical Brit or should I say Scot, I was very wary. However, God had other ideas because when we arrived in the late evening at the guest house where we would be staying, we were met by a lovely man who proceeded to hand me a note to say, "10am tomorrow morning you see the Health Care Practitioner". I was taken aback because firstly I hadn't requested this, and secondly, I was still a little wary. I took the note and just had to say to myself, "Lord, it's over to you, you know best". I slept well that night.

We spent a lovely four days in the Saarland region of Germany and met some lovely people as we found out the background to the Centre which had been in the village for nearly 20 years. It was a very small village of about 400 residents and in the middle of the village was the Guest House and Wellness Centre. Many of the villagers were part of a Christian community that also ran the Centre, so they came and went from the Centre daily. They also had guests staying from all over the world. It was surrounded with forests and orchards with hills in the distance and we were just on the edge of France. A beautiful location.

And so, I met Carina the Health Care Practitioner the following day. Carina had of course many questions to ask, viewing my hospital reports, scans, X-rays, medication and the many supplements I was taking. I had a suitcase just for all this stuff. I was then put on her "magic machine" which through energy frequencies could see deep into the cells and reveal what was going on in my body.

She told me I had two blockages in my spine. That of course was the cancer I knew I had in two places. My liver and kidneys were weak and various other things were needing to be put right.

Carina ended by saying, "I can help you, but I will need you for at least a month." All treatments would be non-invasive and natural.

I said we would go home and think about it and get back to her. She also gave me some idea of cost as well. We returned home both feeling happy, there was something else I could do.

Several weeks passed and Sandy kept asking me what my decision was going to be on going to Germany. I kept saying that I didn't know. To be truthful I was thinking of the cost and when I told him my concerns, he said, "We are in a blessed position, we have a house we can sell and some money in the bank. What is more important, your health or possessions?" That was me told!

I was lying in the bath one day and I said to God, "If you want me to go to Germany you have to show me because I don't know what I'm meant to do." I was scared too, that any treatments might undo the good that had already been done.

Now at that time, Sandy had been mentioning to me for a few months on and off, about a client of his who owed him money for two years work. He tried getting in touch with this gentleman numerous times, through email, text and phone but to no avail. He kept saying, "I just know I'm not going to get paid; he's just not getting back to me."

About three days after my prayer in the bath, Sandy got a phone call from the said gentleman very apologetic and aware that he owed him money and he asked could they meet for lunch the following week, and this was arranged.

The outcome of that lunch was a complete miracle. The client asked Sandy how much he owed him. Sandy told him the amount that was agreed initially but his client wouldn't have that and said, "Sandy, you have done a lot more work on this than was originally envisaged" and increased his payment. Sandy stressed that as far as he was concerned, he was still very happy with what was agreed initially. To cut a long story short, he increased his payment three times! This had never happened before and might, humanly speaking, never happen again. Our God is awesome and does work in mysterious ways.

When Sandy came home and told me what had happened and the amount paid, it was enough for me to go to Germany and for Sandy to get his agreed fee. That was my prayer well and truly answered and I just knew then, there was no turning back. So, two months later I left for Germany to spend the whole of August 2013 over there.

8

You Are Healed!

I remember sitting at the airport waiting to depart to Luxembourg, and thinking *what am I doing? Why am I sitting here? This is crazy.* I don't think I had ever been away for so long from home on my own. Carina had said at least a month at the Centre and so I didn't book a return ticket until I knew how long she would want me, it could be longer but how much longer, I hadn't a clue.

A few days before I left for Germany, my dear friend Jean gave me an envelope and said, "Don't open it till you get to the airport". I had it with me in my hand luggage and so I opened it and inside was an encouraging letter from Jean with a verse of scripture aptly for that time and ensuring me she was with me in prayer. I remember reading the words, "Viv, God has told me you are going to make a complete recovery, He said it, I believe it, it is done!" Wow! What an encouragement. As it turned out, nearly every day whilst in Germany I heard from this amazing woman.

The flight was only an hour, so I didn't have time to think about much but do remember on the plane praying and saying, "Lord, I place myself in your hands, you know what is ahead and I trust in you."

Arriving at Luxembourg airport, I was met by a lovely man with a big smile, Michael, who didn't speak much English so the forty-five minute journey from Luxembourg to Saarland was rather quiet. Some sign language came into play as we journeyed but not very successfully.

Again, when I arrived in the early evening, I was given a very warm welcome and shown to my room where I would be living for the next four weeks. Room 18. A lovely room overlooking the beautiful garden with my own private patio area. Little did I know that room was going to become my little haven. I came to feel a real peace when there and heard God speak to me clearly at various times.

I settled in, had dinner and there I met a young American lady who had arrived that afternoon and just happened to be in the next room to me (again no coincidence). Amber and I became good buddies while we were there. We were both there for the same length of time and were both grateful for each other although the love and friendship we received from the staff was second to none which we both valued greatly.

The next day after breakfast I met again with Carina. Carina gave me my schedule for the week and boy was it full! I began with having nothing but green juice for four days to cleanse my body, a taste that had to be acquired let us say. This was given to me every two to three hours. I have to say, the food there was amazing, in taste, in quantity and in appearance even although we were kept to special foods, all were very tasty. In between, I had various other treatments, too numerous to mention, but all benefitting my body especially in the detoxification process. This was the pattern for the next four weeks.

Sometimes I would feel on top of the world and other times very low and tired, but I was told to expect this. One of the channels on the TV in my room had wonderful relaxing worship music with beautiful scenery and verses of scripture, enough time to read and meditate on before the next one would appear. Very often I would find myself lying on my bed with tears streaming down my face as I meditated on the words as they appeared and listened to the music. These times became very special. A real release.

It was in this room that I had counselling – all part of the holistic approach to the healing process. This was a first for me and of course I didn't have anything to be counselled for...or so I thought. That rather changed when after completing a questionnaire I begun to realise, well, there just might be some things here needing to be dealt with. The process opened much that I didn't even think about but was there although well buried. I was counselled by two wonderful people who told me how to deal with various situations and after intensive prayer, I had to let it all go, through a process. Wow, what a freedom I discovered which I hadn't felt before. This whole experience was not only challenging but life changing.

During my time at the Centre I met several people, not just from Germany, but from all parts of the world. I am still in contact with some even today. Nearly every day someone new would appear and someone would leave. In the evenings after dinner, we would congregate in the lounge area and were blessed to listen to some wonderful musicians, greatly enjoying their music, joining in a singsong and even some dancing. It was all good fun and so good to relax and feel the benefits of the day.

During these times together and over meals we came to know one another better and became a close-knit group looking out for and supporting one another where we could. We were all there for various ailments including burn-out and so it was good to be able to support and encourage one another, especially when we were feeling rubbish!

The staff in the Wellness Centre became very special people to me and to everyone who visited. There were five staff there at that time. The gentle way they treated us, the love they showed to us and the many laughs along the way made the whole experience so wonderful and a time I will never forget. Even when some couldn't speak English and we couldn't speak German, it became interesting and usually ended in laughter or off to find an interpreter. We laughed and cried together.

As I entered my fourth week there, Carina asked to see me. She said, "I think you can book your return flight home in one week's time I feel you are ready to go home, and I will put you back on the machine before you leave". Although I was enjoying my time there to hear this news was a real relief in many ways and a joy in another. So, the return flight home was booked.

On my final day there, I met with Carina in the morning, and she put me on the machine. To me it looked complete gobble-de-gook as the waves went through my body but to her it all meant something. She turned to me with all the other results she had obtained and said, "Now there are no blockages on your spine, go home and get a scan. You are healed!"

The indentation and distortion on my spine was now gone! I can't tell you how I felt, every moment and every pound spent at this point was worth it all and more. I had just heard the words I was waiting to hear. Wow, God, you are so good!

That afternoon, I was given my final treatment, a wonderful body massage. The lovely Dani who had given me a lot of my treatments was booked in to give me my final treatment. This was a whole-body affair, but as I lay back, eyes closed, enjoying the moment, I could hear Dani quietly praying as she gave me the massage.

This was no different to all the other times she treated me but this time there was something more. By the time she had reached my head, I realised she was crying and as she massaged my head, I felt her tears fall on to my face. Wow! This was so powerful, but such was the love and dedication these people had for us. That moment will remain with me for the rest of my life. I should say that all treatments carried out, were covered with prayer, no matter what we were having done.

Sandy had arrived a few days earlier to take me home but also to spend some more time to experience this wonderful place. He couldn't get over how well I looked, and to see I was walking upright. The last time he saw me, I was quite bent over with various aches and pains in my body, especially my back but with the great manipulation and exercise I received I was more upright than I ever had been.

I said my tearful goodbyes to everyone at *His Place*, in many ways reluctantly, and returned to England to arrange for a scan.

9

My Last Hospital Visit

I called the hospital on my return to arrange for a scan on my spine. The Oncologist queried why I wanted a scan and asked if I felt unwell. No way was I going to tell her where I had been! I said I felt as a few months had passed, I would like to know what was going on in my body. And so eventually and very reluctantly, she agreed for me to have another MRI scan.

This scan proved quite interesting. The previous MRI scan lasted about forty minutes but for this one after fifteen minutes the machine stopped and then started and then stopped and then a lady came and pulled me out. As usual, with all my scans, as I was in "the tunnel" I would not just be praying but singing worship songs, the words really helped me keep focused on what was important and gave me that inward peace.

She said she heard me singing, poor lady, I thought I was alone and no-one would be hearing me. She asked what I was singing and when I told her she said, "Well, you sounded very happy." "I am," I said. She then asked me, "What were you told the last time you had your MRI scan?" I replied, "Disease in two parts of my spine." "Just hold on," she said, "I need to just check we have covered everything." Back she came, "You can go now, your Oncologist will be in touch."

I left knowing this lady was confused but felt I couldn't enlighten her. I had a real joy and excitement inside of me at this point.

A week later, I had what turned out to be my last appointment with the Oncologist. She invited me in and asked if I would like to see my scan. I said, "Ok". She showed where there was arthritis up my spine, collapsed vertebrae and then she said, "And that is it!" I said, "And that is it?" Nothing more did she say until I was about to go out of the door, then she said, "It is inevitable it will return somewhere else at some point". I didn't receive that.

I couldn't wait to get out of that room and then I heard Sandy behind me say to her, "we won't be seeing you again" as we walked out, never to return. I think what he meant was my wife is healed so we won't be back, but it could have been taken differently…oops!

I was like Peter and John in the New Testament nearly dancing and singing but certainly praising God as I walked out of that hospital. This was the day I was waiting for since receiving Psalm 91 back in March 2012 and receiving His promise from Philippians, *"I will carry it out to completion"*. And He did. I just want to give God all the glory.

A week later, I received a copy of a letter sent to my GP from the Oncologist, signing me off. No mention of any further scans, strange I thought, and to this day I have never returned to that hospital for scans or visits in relation to cancer.

My next appointment with my GP was a confusing one. We had a long chat. Firstly, he was delighted with my results but very confused I had not been invited for any further scans. "You and me both," I said. I then proceeded to tell him I had just returned from a Wellness Centre in Germany. Up to this point my relationship with my GP had always been great but at that moment I experienced a side I had never seen before. He seemed quite angry. "Why did you do that? Your

Oncologist is going to wash her hands of you," he said. Well, she already had! He was very concerned that I had been "ripped off" and lost a lot of money.

I explained to him that I went there on recommendation, I had also visited and investigated before I went. Also, if you are told there is nothing more the medical profession can do for you, and someone comes along with a possible lifeline, aren't you going to take it? "I see you were pushed into a corner," he replied. At this point he became much calmer, and he became from then on very supportive although he didn't understand what I was doing and didn't seem to want to know.

From then on he just gave me what I wanted when requested, if I tried to tell him why he would stop me and say, "I don't understand it, but keep doing what you're doing, it's working, you have defied all the odds." For me those words were so encouraging, and I thanked the Lord every day, and still do, for my healing.

Following this, once a year I would visit my GP and still do, to arrange for all my bloods to be taken for everything including vitamins and minerals – usually about 10 vials of blood. I want to do this so I can keep some track of how my body is performing. Every year the results come back with no action needed or very little. My GP was astounded, especially after the first year, after all my body had gone through. This was probably because my body had been completely detoxed. Each year he would go over all my results with me (and there were a fair number) and he would be amazed. He would always say, whatever you're doing, it's working, keep at it. Another few words of encouragement, making it feel all worthwhile.

59

10

Ten Years On...

As I was to have no more scans or any support from the hospital, I decided that each year I would return to the clinic in Germany to be checked over and obtain any "top-up" of treatments as needed. I returned every year for six years following my initial month's visit. Before every visit I would get my little envelope from Jean to be opened at the airport or sometimes when I arrived in Germany. Again, every time her message inside was always spot-on and full of encouragement. Jean was a real encourager. Oh, how I miss her.

I really looked forward to these times when I would visit and go on the "magic machine" and find out how things were going within my body, (maybe that part wasn't so exciting as I was always a bit apprehensive until I got the results). After that, I would relax, enjoy the pampering, rejuvenation and bask in the love and peace of that wonderful place. These were the times I would hear from God the most, in the peace and tranquillity of my surroundings.

As I said before, every visit I would meet people from different parts of the world, many I am still in touch with today and some have become very good friends. I can't thank God enough for that place and the wonderful, dedicated staff

He had placed there and, of course, for our friend Paul for telling me about it in the first place. This is undoubtedly all part of God's rich tapestry.

Unfortunately, *His Place* had to close three years ago, and this came as a great disappointment to me. However, I realise that for me it was right for that season, and am very grateful I was given the opportunity and privilege to go there. It was a very, very special place which will always remain close to my heart.

Today, I am looked after by a very good Health Care Practitioner in London, who has the same "magic machine" and keeps an eye on me. There are quite a few more of these machines around now which is good compared to ten years ago. I do miss however, the intensive work and treatments that I received whilst being an in-house guest for a period of a week or two and getting a good check-up into the bargain all at the same time. I still try and get several of the treatments I received in Germany regularly in the UK and look after my body as much as I can. I strongly feel it is my responsibility to do this and certainly no-one else is going to do it for me. I know I fail often but I do my best to keep on top of it, it's the very least I can do.

At this juncture I want to thank and give the glory to the One, I believe, who got me through this journey. His name is Jesus or God if you haven't already noticed. When I look back, I realise I was never left alone and through the many prayers lifted on my behalf, I was led through a process of waiting, hearing and believing, and from that came the many avenues that opened for me.

I never looked for a diet, I never looked for a Wellness Centre anywhere, never mind Germany, I just had to be obedient. God had gone ahead of me as He always does, and I needed to trust Him and keep positive.

His ways are not always our ways, but He knows the end from the beginning and the beginning from the end. It is my prayer that, if you don't already have assurance and a hope then you will find my God who is standing with His arms open wide for you. All you need to do is ask.

What about the future? Well, like every one of us, I don't know what that will look like, but I just take a day at a time and thank God for it and for giving me the last ten years. I am so, so, grateful. Of course, we must be sensible, and plan the future, but nothing is guaranteed, we make these decisions trusting we have made the right ones and for me I can only put my trust in the One who holds the future. Not only in sickness must I trust Him, but also in health must I trust Him. I can do no better. There is no-one better.

To conclude, I need to say this is my journey, my experiences, my beliefs. My beliefs are a free choice, a free gift, and open to all. Two things are certain; we are all born into this world, and we will all leave. What happens in between, however, is different for every one of us, no two lives are identical, we are all unique.

I respect we all have different views and ideas but one thing we can all do is help each other along the way as we journey and I want this book to do just that, to give hope, encouragement and peace of body, soul and spirit.

"This sickness will not end in death. No, it is
for God's glory so that God's Son may be
glorified through it."
John 11:4

To God be the Glory!

If there is anything in this little book
you would like to talk about then please email me;

vivienctaylor@gmail.com

I am always happy to chat.

My Journey…

Left: The 'Three Amigos'. Myself (back left), Heather (back right) and Jean (front).

Below: With my lovely Mum.

Above: With some of my fantastic work colleagues.

Below: Germany – with Simone, Wellness Assistant, following one of my treatments.

Above: *His Place*, Germany, Room 18 – my haven.

Below: The lovely Annie, one of the many people I met at *His Place*.

Above: Sandy coming to take me home after my treatment in Germany.